THIS ROBLOX BOOK BELONGS TO:

NAME: Lara

MY AGE!

MY FAVOURITE ROBLOX GAME IS

FLEE THE FACILITY ✓

PIGGY ✓

ADOPT ME! ✓

JAILBREAK ✓

MURDER MYSTERY 2 ✓

ROYALE HIGH ✓

BUILD A BOAT FOR TREASURE ✓

RESORT TYCOON ✓

MY FAVOURITES!

GAME:
....

MOVIE:
....

TV SHOW:
....

BOOK:
....

MUSIC:
....

ANIMAL:
....

FOOD:
....

DRINK:
....

COLOUR:
....

Published by D.C. Thomson & Co.,Ltd 185 Fleet Street, London EC4A 2HS. © D.C. Thomson, 2023. Whilst every reasonable care will be taken neither D.C. Thomson & Co.,Ltd., nor its agents accept liability for loss or damage to colour transparencies or any other material submitted to this publication. Distributed by Frontline Ltd, Stuart House, St John's St, Peterborough, Cambridgeshire PE1 5DD. Tel: +44 (0) 1733 555161. Website: www. frontlinedistribution.co.uk. EU Representative Office: DC Thomson & Co Ltd, c/o Findmypast Ireland, Irishtown, Athlone, Co. Westmeath, N37 XP52

DC THOMSON
EXPORT DISTRIBUTION (EXCLUDING AU AND NZ) SEYMOUR DISTRIBUTION LTD, 2 EAST POULTRY AVENUE, LONDON EC1A 9PT TEL: +44(0)20 7429 4000 FAX: +44(0)20 7429 4001 WEBSITE: WWW.SEYMOUR.CO.UK

ENQUIRIES: EDITOR@110GAMING.COM

DRAW AN AVATAR!

IT'S BLOX-TASTIC!

GET INTO ROBLOX

ONE GAME, TONS OF COOL CREATIONS!

NOT SURE WHAT TO PLAY?

MeepCity

Hang out with your friends and make MeepCity your own! Buy pets, improve your house, go fishing and more!

Speed Run 4

This game has 32 levels of fun! Go as fast as you can, jump from platform to platform and try not to fall!

DID YOU KNOW?

Roblox lets you play hundreds of different games with your friends. Every game in Roblox was made by other players just like you!

CHECK OUT SOME OF THE BEST GAMES ON ROBLOX!

Work at a Pizza Place

Work fast to make pizzas for people. The better you do, the cooler you can make your house!

Roblox Rocks!

Check out the different types of games in Roblox!

OBBIES

Obbies are obstacle courses! Run fast and jump quickly to make it through.

ELEVATOR   ELEVATORS

Every time the lift stops, you get a new random thing to do!

TYCOON

Tycoon games are all about making lots of money!

HIDE AND SEEK   EXTREME

Find a great hiding spot and hope the other players don't catch you!

GREAT GAME GENERATOR

Find out which Roblox game you should play next

START

You love simulation games!

YES → You can spend hours on a game!

NO →

You're a big puzzle fan!

NO → Roblox is your fave game ever

YES

NO → It's every player for themselves!

ROBLOX ROCKS!

CHOOSE CAREFULLY!

VEHICLE SIMULATOR! //////////

● Drive through the streets in cool supercars in this awesome Roblox game!

YES

You're a sports car fanatic!

YES

You're a big collector!

NO

YES

You're a speed demon!

NO

NO

YES

NO

YES

You're better at hiding than seeking!

YES

TREASURE HUNT SIMULATOR! //////

● Ever dreamt of finding hidden treasure? Then this is the game for you!

TREASURE HUNT SIMULATOR

DISASTER DOME! ///////////

● Enter the Disaster Dome and hide from storms and dragons to survive!

GAME DESIGN STUD

DRAW LIKE A DEV WITH OUR GAME DESIGNER!

WHAT TO DO ☒

▶ Complete each mini task on the opposite page to find out what your game will be like.

▶ Use the results to draw your game here!

MY GAME IS CALLED

1

▶ Use the first letter of your name to decide your game genre.

A-G: TYCOON
H-N: CITY BUILDER
O-T: OBBY
U-Z: ROLEPLAY

2

▶ Flip a coin to find your style.

HEADS: BLOCKY
TAILS: REALISTIC

3

▶ Pick your fave colour to find a theme.

RED: ADVENTURE
YELLOW: SPOOKY
BLUE: RANDOM
GREEN: RETRO

4

▶ Tick the ones you've played to reveal any extra elements in your game.

☑ **MEEPCITY: CARS**
☑ **PIGGY: WEAPONS**
☑ **THEME PARK TYCOON 2: ROLLERCOASTERS**
☑ **ROYALE HIGH: A SCHOOL**
☑ **ADOPT ME!: PETS**

5

▶ Combine a word from each column to name your game.

ACTION	ISLAND
SPEED	RUMBLE
MEGA	BEANS
BLOX	CRAFT
RO	ROYALE

HOW ROBLOX
OBSESSED ARE YOU?

ARE YOU A TOTAL **BLOX** HEAD? PICK YOUR CHOICES TO FIND OUT!

1 The first thing you think about when you wake up is...

1 Roblox.

2 Breakfast... duh!

2 Do you own any Roblox merch?

1 Everything I own is Roblox themed!

2 Maybe a t-shirt at the back of my cupboard...

3 If Roblox no longer existed, you would:

1 Create your own version of Roblox!

2 Find something else to play.

5 On your Christmas list this year is...

1 A Robux gift card.

2 A new skateboard.

4 If you had a puppy, you'd call it...

1 Obby.

2 Steve.

SIT, STEVE!

6 What would you rather watch on YouTube?

1 Ethan Gamer's Roblox **Let's Plays.**

2 Stampy's Minecraft **vids.**

MOSTLY RED
YOUR LOVE FOR THE GAME IS *NEXT LEVEL!* IF IT'S NOT ROBLOX, IT'S JUST NOT WORTH IT!

HALF & HALF
YOU ENJOY ROBLOX – BUT YOU LIKE PLAYING OTHER GAMES JUST AS MUCH.

MOSTLY BLUE
YOU DON'T REALLY GET WHAT ALL THE HYPE IS ABOUT – MINECRAFT IS MUCH BETTER.

BLOXY BINGO

TICK OFF EACH CHALLENGE AS YOU COMPLETE IT!

EARNED A BADGE! ✓

MADE YOUR OWN GAME! ✓

BEAT YOUR MATES! ✓

TOP OF THE BLOX!

CUSTOMISED YOUR AVATAR! ✓

DELIVERED A PIZZA! ✓

FLOWN A HELICOPTER! ✓

ADOPTED A PET! ✓

BUILT A HOUSE! ✓

JUMPED PLAYING PIGGY! ✓

PLAYED IN AN ELEVATOR! ✓

COMPLETED AN OBBY! ✓

STOLEN A CAR! ✓

BATTLED A MONSTER! ✓

SPENT AGES PICKING A GAME! ✓

BUMPED INTO A YOUTUBER! ✓

All About OBBIES

EVERYTHING YOU NEED TO KNOW!

WHAT IS IT?

The word obby is short for 'obstacle course'. These games tend to involve a lot of running, jumping and great gaming reflexes! If you love platformer games like Mario, Sonic and Crash Bandicoot, then obbies are for you.

HOW TO PLAY!

Sometimes you have to fail if you want to win! Each time you try out a new obby, there'll be parts of the course you might not know how to do straight away and that's OK. Any time you lose, you'll be able to learn from what went wrong and beat it next time!

TOP TYPES!

Obbies come in all different varieties, meaning no two obbies will be exactly the same. Some obbies have a storyline where you uncover more of the story the further you get, where other obbies might be escape-themed, or even just loads of levels for you to master!

TICK THE GAMES YOU'VE PLAYED!

GREAT ESCAPES
Some of our fave escape obbies!

- ☐ Escape the Dungeon
- ☐ Escape School
- ☑ Escape Running Head

LEVEL UP

How far can you get?

- ☐ Super Fun Obby
- ☐ Speed Run 4
- ☑ Mega Easy Obby

PLAY

SO RANDOM

These games are so weird!

- ☐ Grumpy Gran
- ☐ Mr Stinky's Detention
- ☐ Baby Bobby's Daycare

EPIC OBBIES!

AWESOME!

10

9

8

7

6

GREAT

5

4

3

2

1

COOL

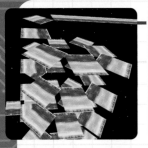

SPEED RUN 4

■ Speed Run 4 is a fun parkour challenge with a seemingly endless number of levels. When you think you've finished it, you'll usually unlock another dimension! Can you beat them all?

OUR RATING: 10

YOUR RATING:

THE DROPPER

■ The Dropper started out in Minecraft, but then moved to Roblox! It has over 120 unique levels and counting, so it'll keep you busy for ages.

OUR RATING: 9

YOUR RATING:

THE FLOOR IS LAVA

■ Uh-oh – in this game you have to complete over ten obstacle courses while lava is rising and trying to take you out! Can you do them all, or will the lava get you?

OUR RATING: 8

YOUR RATING: 6

BARRY'S PRISON RUN

■ Barry's Prison Run is a really cool first-person adventure that has weapons and boss fights. It is a bit short, though! If you like it, be sure to check out @PlatinumFalls other games!

OUR RATING: 7

YOUR RATING: 7

MEGA EASY OBBY

■ Good, simple fun! Once you've mastered this one, you can move on to something a bit more challenging or you can even use this one as a parkour warm-up!

OUR RATING: 6

YOUR RATING: 9

ROBLOX RANDOMISER!

All about obbies or is it time for a tycoon?

1 Who is your favourite superhero?

- **A** Iron Man ☐
- **B** Batman ☐
- **C** Spider-Man ☐

2 What is your favourite non-Roblox game?

- **A** Minecraft ☐
- **B** Super Mario ☐
- **C** LEGO Worlds ☐

3 What would you buy with a million pounds?

- **A** Your own shop ☐
- **B** A bouncy castle ☐
- **C** A circus ☐

4 What is your favourite way to play games?

- **A** Tablet ☐
- **B** Console ☐
- **C** PC ☐

5 Who is your favourite celeb?

- **A** Simon Cowell ☐
- **B** Usain Bolt ☐
- **C** Ant & Dec ☐

MOSTLY A...
YOU SHOULD PLAY A TYCOON!

- If you love having the fanciest clothes and the newest tech, then you'll love building up your empire in a Roblox tycoon map!

MOSTLY B...
YOU SHOULD PLAY AN OBBY!

- Gotta go fast! Running, jumping and sliding are your favourite things and you're always ready for a new challenge!

MOSTLY C...
YOU SHOULD PLAY AN ELEVATOR!

- You're weird, random and proud of it! In a Roblox elevator level you get a new game every time the doors open!

HEROES OF ROBLOXIA GUIDE!

KNOW YOUR HERO!

THERE ARE FIVE TYPES OF HERO, EACH WITH THEIR OWN ABILITIES THAT YOU CAN SWITCH TO AT ANY TIME!

CAPTAIN ROBLOX

● With super strength, Captain Roblox is who you want to use in a fight!

AMETHYSTO

● He was the villain Darkmatter, but now he's a hero who can shoot plasma and make shields!

TESSLA

● Tessla is shockingly cool, especially when you need to zap something!

OVERDRIVE

● No-one can keep up with his speed, not to mention he can throw discs as weapons!

KINETIC

● Kinetic's telekinesis and levitation can be really useful when you need to move something!

KNOW YOUR VILLAIN!

● Cosminus is an evil ruler from another planet who wants to crash the moon into Earth! Here are our top tips on how to stop him!

I RULE!

1. USE CAPTAIN ROBLOX TO FIGHT OFF THE SCIENTISTS!

2. USE KINETIC TO GET TO HARD-TO-REACH PLACES!

3. MOVE AWAY FROM THE SCIENTISTS BEFORE YOU THROW OVERDRIVE'S DISCS!

COSMAZE!

COSMINUS IS ESCAPING THE LAB! QUICK, HELP OVERDRIVE CATCH UP TO HIM!

IT'S NOT OVER!

START

YOU CAN'T CATCH ME!

FINISH

WHAT DO SUPERHEROES PUT IN THEIR DRINKS?

JUST ICE!

ANSWER:

23

CITY LIVING!

BUILD YOUR OWN DREAM ROBLOX WORLD WITH THESE GREAT GAMES!

MEEPCITY

Hang out with your mates and build your dream estate in MeepCity! With loads of minigames to play, an awesome avatar editor and the most adorable Meeps to adopt, there's always something fun to get up to in this epic experience.

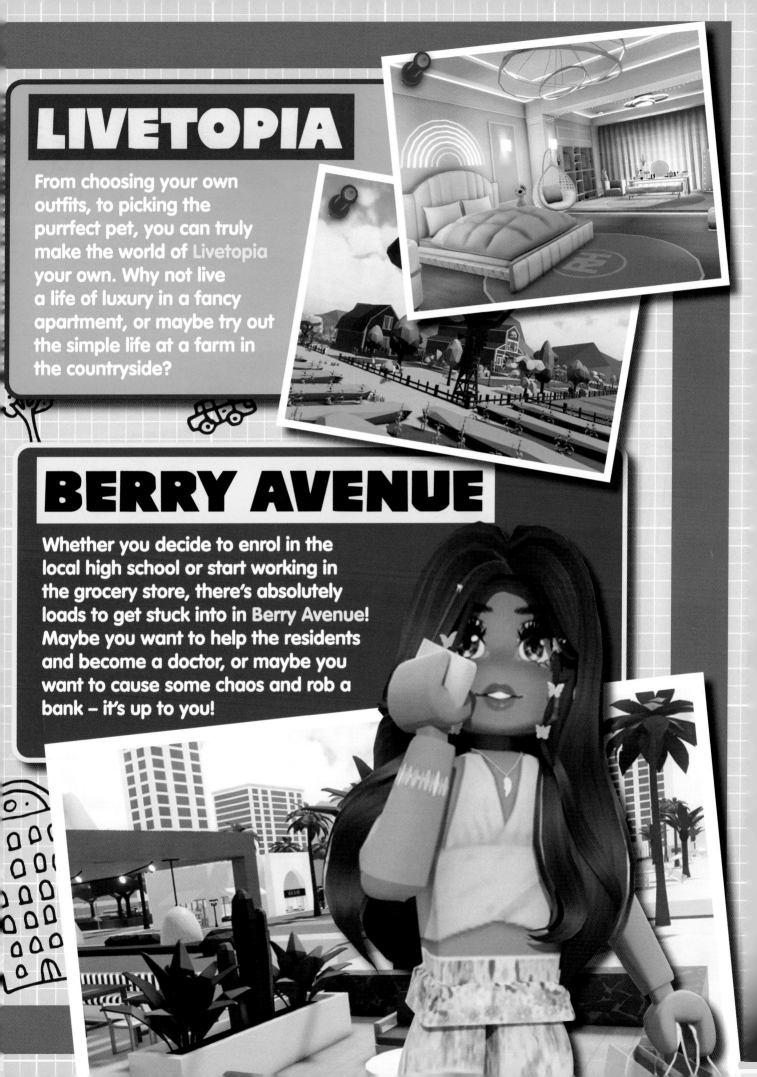

LIVETOPIA

From choosing your own outfits, to picking the purrfect pet, you can truly make the world of Livetopia your own. Why not live a life of luxury in a fancy apartment, or maybe try out the simple life at a farm in the countryside?

BERRY AVENUE

Whether you decide to enrol in the local high school or start working in the grocery store, there's absolutely loads to get stuck into in Berry Avenue! Maybe you want to help the residents and become a doctor, or maybe you want to cause some chaos and rob a bank – it's up to you!

REDCLIFF CITY

Roleplay your way and make Redcliff City your own! You could drive and explore in a super-cool sports car, invite your friends to tour the home of your dreams, or even put on a fashion show with loads of amazing accessories.

EMERGENCY RESPONSE: LIBERTY COUNTY

If you want a world jam-packed full of action, look no further! There are so many different roles to play as, from a heroic firefighter to a criminal on the run so there's always a fun new way to play. With a huge world to explore, there's loads to discover – including a secret mountain hideout!

PURRFECT PET PICKER!

WHERE WILL YOU FIND YOUR DREAM PETS?

START

Your perfect pet is...

— Cute → **You'd rather...**

— Unique → **You love telling jokes.**

You'd rather...
- Customise your home → **You like teaching your pet tricks.**
- Travel unique lands → **Choose an activity:**

You love telling jokes.
- Always → **Choose an activity:**
- Sometimes → **Minigames are...**

Choose an activity:
- Painting → **You like teaching your pet tricks.**
- Go-karting → **Minigames are...**

You like teaching your pet tricks.
- Yes → **Your dream pet is a...**
- Not really → **What best describes you?**

Minigames are...
- Not my thing → **What best describes you?**
- So much fun → **You love customising your pets.**

What best describes you?
- Adventurous → **PET SIMULATOR X**
- Imaginative → **You love customising your pets.**

Your dream pet is a...
- Penguin → **ADOPT ME!**
- Frost dragon → **PET SIMULATOR X**

You love customising your pets.
- Not really → **PET SIMULATOR X**
- Yes → **MEEP CITY**

Penguin

ADOPT ME!

Why have one pet, when you can have loads! From axolotls to unicorns, you have what it takes to level-up all kinds of animal companions.

PET SIMULATOR X

You might be easy-going, but you're always up for an adventure! Collecting lots of pets and travelling to different worlds is your idea of fun.

FISH
FISH

MEEP CITY

Meeps are unique and loyal making them the perfect pets for you! You'll have the best time together hanging out in MeepCity.

BLOX THE DIFFERENCE!

■ Can you find all six differences between the two pictures below?

JOKE ALERT!

What did the cop say to his belly button?

You're under a vest!

YOU STOLE THAT FROM ME!

ANSWERS

29

Speech bubble: FRASER2THEMAX HERE!

FRASER2
MEET THE ROBLOX SUPERSTAR

FRASER 2 THE MAX

NAME: Fraser2TheMax
SUBS: 69.3K
PLAYS: Lots of Roblox!

HOW DID YOU GET INTO ROBLOX?

"I was looking for cool games to play and I came across it. MeepCity is my favourite!"

FRASER2THEMAX AND THE MEEPCITY MYSTERY
? BLOXREVIEW

HOW DID IT FEEL TO BE THE ROBLOX STREAMER OF THE WEEK?

"Amazing, I was really happy to be picked considering my age."

DID YOU KNOW?

Fraser presented an award at the Roblox Bloxy Awards

WHAT'S THE MOST RANDOM THING THAT EVER HAPPENED TO YOU IN ROBLOX?

"I was filming a video and ThnxCya turned up and was also filming a vid but I thought it was a fake ThnxCya... until I watched the vid on his channel and there I was!"

We made it to the deck! lets get to the emergency zipwire!

Award: HARDEST ROBLOX GAME
Now Presenting: Fraser2TheMax

THE MAX

MEEPCITY RACING

FRASER'S No.1 ROBLOX TIP!

"Stay near the edges in MeepCity Racing and if you ever come across a point where you have the choice of a lucky block or a speed boost, go for the speed boost!"

WHAT HAS MADE YOU LOL MOST WHILST GAMING?

"When doing a collab with SallyGreenGamer she got stuck in a secret room I showed her because the item she was wearing was too big to get out the door!"

CHECK OUT FRASER'S CHANNEL AT F2TM.COM

SHREK OR MINIONS?
"Shrek!"

TV OR YOUTUBE?
"YouTube."

BATMAN OR SUPERMAN?
"Batman!"

MINECRAFT OR ROBLOX?
"Roblox!"

DONUT OR ICE CREAM?
"Donut!"

IRON MAN OR SPIDER-MAN?
"Iron Man!"

BATHE IN BAKED BEANS OR SWIM IN MUD?
"Bathe in baked beans!"

YouTube/F2TM

FRASER2THEMAX

ROBLOX ROUND UP!

GAME: FORGET YOUR FRIEND'S BIRTHDAY

WHAT IS IT?

"In this game you wake up to realise you haven't got your friend a birthday cake! Or any presents for that matter! Luckily, you're a great friend (even though you forgot), so you must quickly scramble to get the best cake and coolest gift for their birthday. On your quest you can solve puzzles, find secrets, and explore the world!"

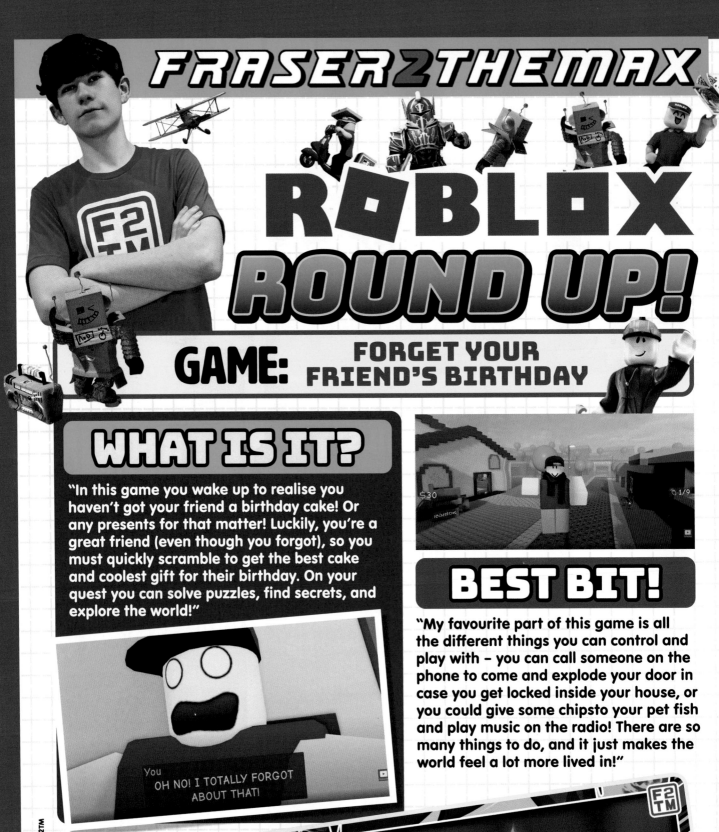

You
OH NO! I TOTALLY FORGOT ABOUT THAT!

BEST BIT!

"My favourite part of this game is all the different things you can control and play with – you can call someone on the phone to come and explode your door in case you get locked inside your house, or you could give some chipsto your pet fish and play music on the radio! There are so many things to do, and it just makes the world feel a lot more lived in!"

CHECK IT OUT!

Scan the code to see Fraser in action!

YouTube/F2TM

GAME: SURVIVE THE END OF ROBLOX

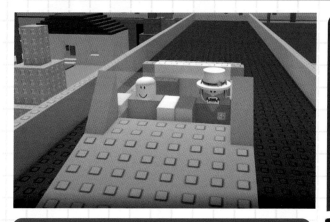

WHAT IS IT?

"In this game, you're chilling in a beautiful Robloxian city when suddenly disaster strikes, and every bad thing imaginable happens! Buildings collapse, volcanoes erupt, and nukes go off! It's your goal to survive and escape the island!"

BEST BIT!

"My favourite part of the game is the players! A lot of the people who play the game take it very seriously and you can have good fun playing with friends. If – when disaster strikes – one of them gets hit with a boulder, a tear may even fall down your eye! I had a fantastic time playing it and made an awesome friend."

CHECK IT OUT!

Scan the code to see Fraser in action!

MAKE A BREAK FOR IT!

F2TM

Ask an adult before using in-game chats and stay safe online!

ROBLOX VS.

SO RANDOM

No-one wants to get bored playing their fave game, so mixing it up with fresh new modes and fun things to try is key!

ROBLOX
Hundreds of experiences to play through, from obbys to tycoons to battle royales.

FALL GUYS
Brand-new seasons every 2-3 months with new skins, maps and themes.

WINNER: ROBLOX!
As much as we love a fresh Fall Guys update, there are just so many games to choose from that Roblox has to take the W!

AWESOME OBSTACLES

Every epic obstacle course should have a mix of amazing - and challenging - activities that will keep you playing again and again!

ROBLOX
Platform jumps
Fake paths
Lava jumps
Speedruns

FALL GUYS
Hex-A-Gone
Slime Climb
Door Dash
Jump Club

WINNER: FALL GUYS!
Sorry Roblox, as much as we love trying to master 99.999% of your obbys, we know we're going to have so much fun tackling every Fall Guys map – even if we're losing!

FALL GUYS

THE OBBY AWARDS!

LOADSA LOLS

Is there anything greater than a healthy dose of the gaming giggles with your best mates? Nah, we didn't think so either!

ROBLOX

Giant butts, millions of memes, poop parkour... Roblox is home to the silliest of the silly and we love it!

FALL GUYS

From Big Yeetus to funny fails and crazy costumes, Fall Guys is guaranteed to make you laugh out loud!

WINNER: DRAW!

We can't decide! Both games are so hilarious in their own way, it's only fair to call it a tie. Sorry, not sorry!

COOL CUSTOMS

Pick the game that you think has the sickest skins and deserves to take the crown!

WHO'S YOUR WINNER?

ROBLOX   **FALL GUYS**

PIZZA DELIVERY DIARY!

HERE'S A SLICE OF ELLIOT'S PIZZA DELIVERING LIFE!

7AM — Time for breakfast! Leftover pizza always tastes better in the morning!

10AM — Morning cartoons = Teenage Mutant Ninja Turtles. We've loads in common, apart from the teenage, mutant, ninja or turtle bit... But they love pizza almost as much as I do!

1PM — If I make a pizza at home and then put it on my own table, have I delivered a pizza to myself? This is really one of the big questions in my life.

4PM — I watched two customers arguing over whether pineapple should go on a pizza. Of course, it should! Gotta get that five a day in somehow!

I WANT A PIZZA THE ACTION!

9PM — I'm at work delivering pizzas all night. If I don't get there in 30 minutes or less, the customers will get them free! I better stop writing about pizza so much and make some delicious deliveries instead!

PIZZA DELIVERY!

CAN YOU BRING THE PIZZA TO THE HUNGRY CUSTOMERS?

 START

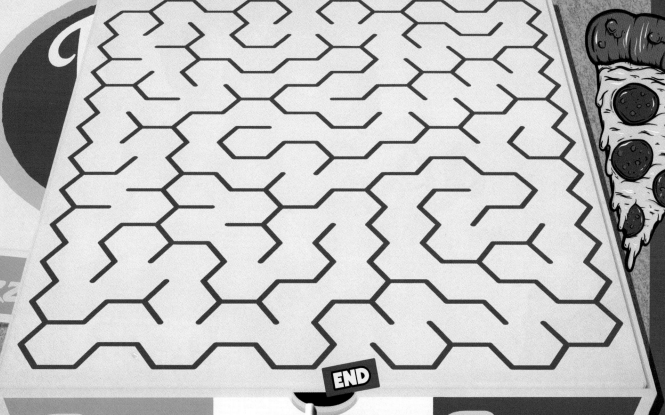

END

Pizza   Pizza

IT'S A PIZZA PARTY!

ADOPT ME!

ADOPT 'EM ALL!

THE GAME:
Families... but with little pets to collect!

THE EXTRAS:
▶ Chores to help your pets grow.

▶ Customisable houses to live in.

▶ Fun events to keep things fresh.

LET'S BE PENG PALS!

ADOPT ME!

HOT TIPS:

KIDS RULE!
To earn extra money, switching to a child lets you complete additional chores to take care of yourself!

GROWTH SPURTS!
Common pets grow up way faster, so if you're looking to get an adult quickly, stick with the easy ones!

RAPID NEONS!
If there is an event with pets available, collect loads of the cheapest and easiest pets – you can use them to make super-rare neons really quickly!

RATINGS
Colour in your stats for Adopt Me!

COOLNESS	
SKILL	
FUN	
OVERALL	

WHO WINS? YOU DECIDE!

PET SIMULATOR X

PERFECT PETS!

PAWSOME!

THE GAME:

Animals... but they're miners?!

THE EXTRAS:

▶ Lots of unique lands to travel to.

▶ Tradeable pets and items.

▶ Rewards to unlock through progress.

RATINGS
Colour in your stats for Pet Simulator X.

- **COOLNESS**
- **SKILL**
- **FUN**
- **OVERALL**

HOT TIPS:

KEEP ON HATCHIN'!
The more eggs you hatch, the better your mastery will become, and a high mastery can get you discounts on super-expensive eggs!

MORE THE MERRIER!
Collecting coins can be easy peezy if you have a buddy. Not only does it give you a coin boost, but it also can be more fun!

LUCK IS ON YOUR SIDE!
When trying to get rarer pets, make sure to have luck boosts enabled so you can increase your odds of getting a super-rare and awesome new pet!

MAKE A ROBLOX GAME!

GETTING STARTED!

"Install Roblox Studio, then go to Roblox.com/create and click on Start Creating. Click New in the panel on the left, then click on Baseplate to open up a new project file. Make sure you have the Explorer and Properties windows open. If you don't see them, click on the View tab in the menu at the top to select them."

Studio

Make Anything You Can Imagine
With our FREE and immersive creation engine

Start Creating

Manage my games

ROBLOX STUDIO IS FREE ON WINDOWS AND MAC!

SPAWN AREA!

STEP 1 "Build a Lobby area where players will spawn by clicking the Home tab, then the Part button. To make the part big enough, set the Size to 35,1,35 in the Properties tab."

STEP 2 "Click on the Model tab, and then click Spawn in Gameplay. This will insert a SpawnLocation. Use the Move and Scale tools to position your SpawnLocation on top of the Part so it's big enough for multiple players to spawn at once."

STEP 3 "Delete the Baseplate so players can't walk on it and cheat the obby! Select the Baseplate inside the Explorer panel and then right click and click Delete."

IMPORTANT! MAKE SURE ALL PARTS ARE ANCHORED, SO THEY DON'T FALL OUT OF THE MAP WHEN THE GAME LOADS! SELECT EACH PART IN THE EXPLORER PANEL AND TICK THE ANCHORED PROPERTY.

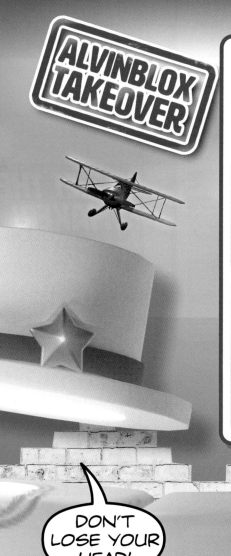

JUMP SET!

STEP 1 "To make your first obstacle, select the part underneath the SpawnLocation, then right click and select Duplicate. Use the move tool to drag it away. This will create a clone of the part which we can now scale down into a jump. Select the Scale tool and drag the handles until it looks more like a rectangle."

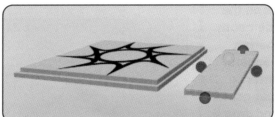

STEP 2 "When you've created your first jump, you can keep Duplicating and moving them along until you have a set. To finish this obstacle, select the platform at the start, duplicate it and move it to the end of the jumps."

DON'T LOSE YOUR HEAD!

CHOOSE PATH!

STEP 1 "Insert a new part into the game, then click and drag it so it's against the platform we just created. Use the Scale tool to make it a long path which you can walk across. Repeat this two more times so you have three paths next to each other."

STEP 2 "Click on each path, then set its CanCollide property to either be checked or unchecked. If it's checked then the player will be able to walk over it. If it is unchecked, they will fall through it! You should have two unchecked paths and one checked path."

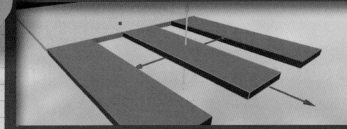

SELECT A PART AND CHANGE THE BRICKCOLOR OR COLOR PROPERTY TO CHANGE ITS COLOUR!

BALL JUMPS!

STEP 1

"Add another platform to separate this obstacle by duplicating the one from the previous step. Then, click on the arrow underneath the Part button and click Sphere. This will insert a ball into our game. Scale it and drag it to where you want the jump to be."

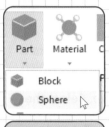

STEP 2

"Duplicate the ball, then use the Move tool to position it away from the first one. Repeat as many times as you like. Make sure that the gap isn't too big and that it's still possible to jump from one ball to the other. Move the balls to the left or right to add more challenge."

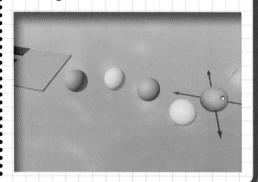

FINISHING TOUCHES!

STEP 1

"Add one more part and scale it so that it's big enough to fit multiple players on. This is going to be the winners' section, where you can hang out once you've completed the obby!"

STEP 2

"You can decorate your winners' section by adding models from the Toolbox. Click the Toolbox button in the Home tab of the Menu and search for a model. Once you've found one you'd like to insert, just click it and it will insert itself into your game. Use the Move and Scale tools to position it in place."

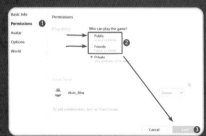

STEP 3

"To publish your game to Roblox, click the File button in the top left corner and then click Publish to Roblox As. Give it a name and add a description if you wish, then click Create. Once published, click Close, then click Game Settings in the Home tab of the menu. Under the Permissions tab, set the Playability to Public or Friends. If you only want your Roblox friends to be able to play the game you can set it to Friends only, or Public if you want anyone to be able to play it. Then click the Save button."

NOW YOU CAN FIND YOUR GAME ON ROBLOX AND PLAY IT!

HAVE A GOOD KNIGHT!

ROBLOX WORLDS

PLAN A ROBLOX TRIP!

TICK THE WORLD WHERE YOU WOULD LIVE AND CROSS THE ONES YOU'D AVOID!

BOOK OF MONSTERS

Whether you're visiting as a human or a monster, there's tonnes of action! Destruction and lots of it is guaranteed as you fight for survival. With limited lives, it feels like the rounds don't last long but it'll keep you coming back for more!

⊕ **Variety of maps and monsters**
⊖ **Limited number of lives**

RAINBOW FRIENDS

It's an amusement park but it feels more like a haunted house! Don't let their names fool you, the Rainbow Friends should be avoided. The field trip to Odd World is one you'll never forget!

⊕ **An unforgettable experience**
⊖ **Rainbow Friends aren't friendly**

ARE YOU FEELING BLUE?

NATURAL DISASTER SURVIVAL

Earthquakes, sandstorms and meteor showers don't make for a relaxing trip, but there's still fun to be had! The view from the Spawning Tower is also pretty cool. If you're a thrill seeker, this is the perfect place for you.

⊕ **Incredible views**
⊖ **Can be intense**

SCUBA DIVING AT QUIL LAKE

There's SO much to explore while discovering the mysteries at Quil Lake! The scenery changes so much under the sea that it never gets boring. Just watch out for underwater lava – it still burns!

⊕ Loads to explore
⊖ Watch out for lava

JETPACK JUMPERS

For something simple but fun, Jetpack Jumpers is the place to be! Stepping on the launch pad and whizzing through the air is such a thrill – but you will crash land eventually!

⊕ Flying with jetpacks is awesome
⊖ Crash landing is common

JOKE ALERT!

WHAT DOES A ROBLOXIAN WEAR ON THEIR FEET? RO-SOCKS!

CITY CREATOR!

DESIGN YOUR VERY OWN ROBLOX WORLD!

MY WORLD IS CALLED: ....

READY TO

ROUND 1

WORK AT A PIZZA PLACE **VS.** THEME PARK TYCOON 2

WELCOME TO BLOXBURG **VS.** MEEPCITY

WINNER! **WORK AT A PIZZA PLACE**
Although we love designing epic theme park rides, Work at a Pizza Place is an all-time Roblox classic! It's like Overcooked meets The Sims — we love it!

WINNER! **WELCOME TO BLOXBURG**
MeepCity is so much fun and there's loads to do, but there's even more to do in Bloxburg! Design your own house, hop in a cool car, or just chill with mates – you can do it all!

ROUND 2

WORK AT A PIZZA PLACE

VS.

WELCOME TO BLOXBURG

WINNER! **WELCOME TO BLOXBURG**
As much as we love making pizza with our mates and doing up our cool house, Bloxburg just has so much more to do in it – it's huge!

ULTIMATE SHOWDOWN!

WELCOME TO BLOXBURG VS

Hanging out with your mates, designing the coolest house ever and driving around the city in sick cars is so much fun but is it as exciting as chasing escaped criminals or breaking out of jail and flying around in helicopter? Nah, we didn't thi so either – sorry Bloxburg!

RUMBLE!

D-TO-HEAD! WHICH ONE WILL WIN?

JAILBREAK VS. **MURDER MYSTERY 2**

WINNER! **JAILBREAK**

Ah, this was a close one! These games are super similar, but Jailbreak is just so exciting! With boats, helicopters and epic map locations, Jailbreak rocks!

ARSENAL VS. **PHANTOM FORCES**

WINNER! **PHANTOM FORCES**

It's the ultimate battle of the shooters! Arsenal's golden knife is cool, but we're going with Phantom Forces. It's packed full of epic maps, weapons and more!

JAILBREAK

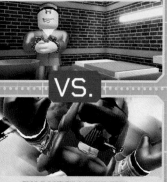

VS.

PHANTOM FORCES

WINNER! **JAILBREAK**

Both games can be action-packed, filled with chaos and excitement, but Jailbreak offers more than just cool combat. From planning heists to epic escapes, it's wild!

JAILBREAK

WINNER!

WE'RE NUMBER ONE AND ON THE RUN!

COOLEST CARS!

AWESOME

10

ECLAIRE

■ What the Eclaire lacks in its handling, it makes up for with a really high top speed and a general cool factor thanks to its sleek two colour design. It also gets extra points as the first car in Jailbreak to have a 3D interior!

OUR RATING: 10

YOUR RATING:

9

8

ROADSTER

■ The Roadster has the highest acceleration in Jailbreak, making it a go-to choice for cops and criminals alike. If the cops don't have one and you do, you've basically already escaped!

OUR RATING: 9

YOUR RATING:

7

LA MATADOR

■ Added to Jailbreak in the Supercar Update, the La Matador is a cheap car that can reach some incredible speeds. It's faster than the Ferrari, which is twice as expensive!

OUR RATING: 8

YOUR RATING:

6

GREAT
5

STALLION

■ The Stallion is a fast car with good handling. It's also really sleek looking, so if you have one you'll be getting away quickly and looking stylish, all at once!

OUR RATING: 7

YOUR RATING:

4

3

VOLT BIKE

■ Thanks to its high acceleration and small size, the Volt Bike is a great choice for escaping from the police!

OUR RATING: 7

YOUR RATING:

2

1

COOL

MAKE MR. ROBOT HEAD!

You're gonna want to make this!

WHAT YOU NEED:
- BROWN CARDBOARD BOX
- 2 PAPER BOWLS
- TINFOIL
- 3 BENDY STRAWS
- BLACK MARKER PEN
- PVA GLUE

1 ● Scrunch up some tin foil to make three balls then use more foil to wrap the paper bowls and straws. Make sure to bend the straws into L-shapes first.

DO THIS ACTIVITY UNDER THE SUPERVISION OF A PARENT OR GUARDIAN.

2 ● Insert the end of a straw into a tinfoil ball to make an antenna. Wrap more tinfoil around the ball and straw to hold them in place. Now make two more.

3 ● Carefully poke a hole in the middle of both paper bowls with a pen, then push the short end of the straw in. Use clear tape or more foil to secure it. Glue each bowl to the ends of the box.

4 ● Poke the last straw into the top of the box to make the final antenna. Use tape to stick the bottom of the straw to the inside of the box. Finally, use a black marker to draw the face and buttons!

GET SPOOKED!

PREPARE FOR A SCARE WITH THESE CREEPY GAMES!

SPIDER

Solve puzzles, collect keys and avoid the Spider as you try to escape each map without being bitten! Each round, a different player will take a turn at playing as the Spider but with loads of different skins to choose from, you can totally make this creepy crawly your own!

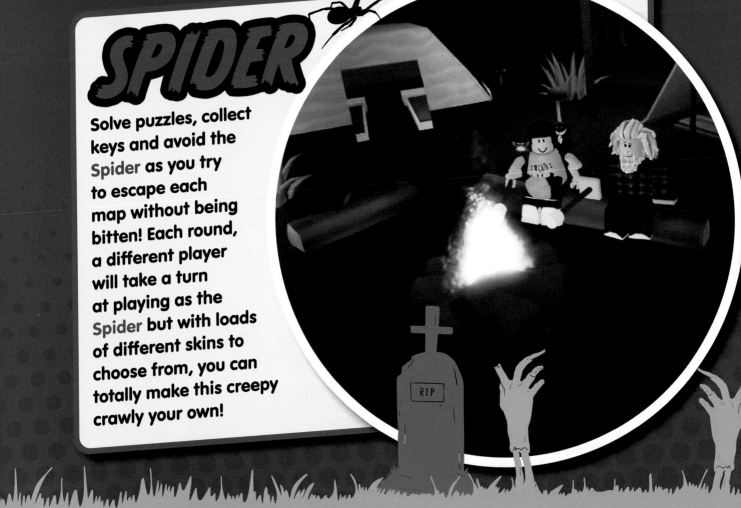

PIGGY

Play your way through each chapter of this spooky story, uncovering the game's mysteries as you go. With a whole host of different game modes to choose, from Infection to Tag, as well as two books to play through, Piggy will keep you on the edge of your seat for ages!

RAINBOW FRIENDS

This might look like a cute and colourful game, but don't be fooled! When your trip to a theme park goes wrong, you must collect items to get through each night and escape the creepy Rainbow Friends!

RIVERRIDE THROUGH
HEMLOCK
WOODS

DOORS

Explore the hotel and work your way through rooms one to 100 on your mission to escape! Each room you enter is randomly generated, so you'll never have the same experience twice as you work your way through. Watch out for who might be lurking behind each door!

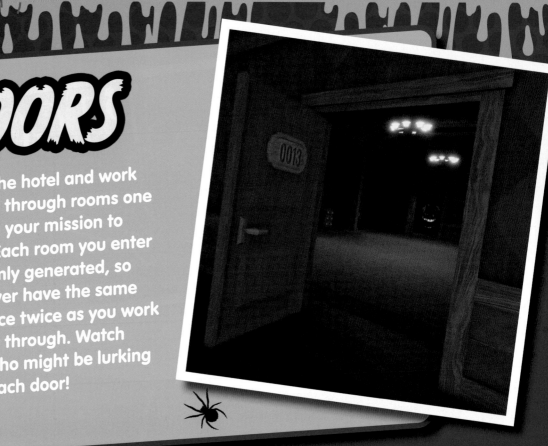

APEIROPHOBIA

You never know what to expect from Apeirophobia's creepy levels! Will they be safe? Will they be scary? Solve the puzzles and find out for yourself! The more you play and get to know the different entities, the longer you'll last next time you log on.

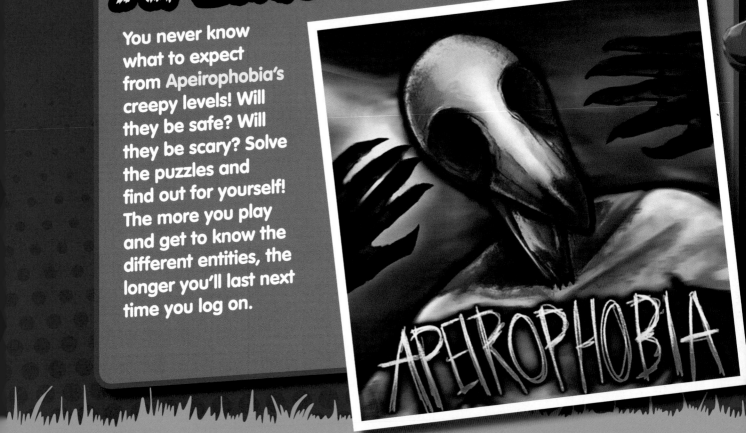

FLEE THE FACILITY

Can you avoid the Beast and escape the map without being frozen?! Hack computers, unlock doors, hide and sneak your way out of the facility. Or, you can take a turn playing as the Beast, using your special hammer to freeze foes!

IT'S HAMMER TIME!

MEGA PUZZLES

PUT YOUR PUZZLING SKILLS TO THE TEST!

JAILBREAKERS!
Can you escape Roblox jail?

START

FINISH

SPOT THE DIFFERENCE!

Find all five differences between the two pics below!

WORD BLOX!

- ◪ GRAVITYCOIL
- ◪ HAT
- ◪ ROBUX
- ◪ OBBY
- ◪ GEAR
- ◪ AVATAR
- ◪ TYCOON
- ◪ ROBLOX

F	L	H	V	H	J	A	V	A	T	A	R
G	R	A	V	I	T	Y	C	O	I	L	D
M	T	T	F	R	J	Q	X	V	Y	Y	S
B	L	Y	B	N	W	N	U	U	C	B	F
I	U	P	H	J	D	L	B	K	L	S	Z
D	B	T	M	D	H	R	O	B	L	O	X
G	I	Y	S	Q	E	Q	R	F	I	I	D
B	R	C	Z	W	K	R	Y	D	Q	W	T
Q	R	O	W	B	R	G	E	A	R	J	J
L	R	O	Y	L	G	K	M	R	Q	H	R
Q	H	N	D	M	P	C	V	Y	F	E	D
T	G	Q	U	O	B	B	Y	K	J	J	U

ODD BLOX OUT!

Which of these is NOT one of the main heroes in Heroes of Robloxia?

CAPTAIN ROBLOX ☐
OVERDRIVE ☐
FAKEBLOX ☐

ANSWERS

ODD BLOX OUT!
Fakeblox

SPOT THE DIFFERENCE!

WORD BLOX!

JAILBREAKERS!

ROBLOX IS ONE OF THE BEST GAMES AROUND!

8 REASONS

ROBLOX ROCKS!

1 YOU CAN MAKE GAMES!

Check out Roblox Studio to make your very own games! With loads of drag and drop options and re-made objects, you

5 YOU CAN PLAY IT ANYWHERE!

Roblox is on PC, Mac, Xbox, tablets and even mobile phones – so whether you're at home or you're on the go,

FREE!

- Roblox doesn't have to cost anything! If you're happy not to spend, you never have to!

7 YOU CAN CUSTOMISE YOUR AVATAR!

- There are so many ways to change up your avatar and show off your unique sense of style!

8 THERE'S SO MUCH TO DO!

- Roblox has games for everyone – no matter what you're interested in, there'll be something for you!

ALL AGES!

- With loads of epic games to play and explore, everyone is bound to find a game they'll love – even your gran!

3 THERE ARE VIRTUAL WORLDS!

- Many Roblox games have gigantic online worlds to explore, so it really feels like you're on an awesome adventure!

4 THE GREAT COMMUNITY!

- Roblox gamers are some of the nicest around!

HIT LIST!

Have you played these Roblox hits? Tick the boxes next to the games you've played!

NATURAL DISASTER SURVIVAL

THEME PARK TYCOON 2

JAILBREAK

HIDE AND SEEK

HIDE AND SEEK EXTREME

ALL STAR TOWER DEFENCE

SONIC SPEED SIMULATOR

SPIN A STORY!

SPIN A PENCIL THREE TIMES TO FIND OUT...

WRITE YOUR OWN ROBLOX ADVENTURE!

1 Where your story takes place.

2 One thing that happens in your story.

3 Who your main character is.

1 BLOXBURG

1 SURROUNDED BY LAVA

1 RACETRACK

2 A mysterious egg appears

2 Someone adopts a magical dragon

2 Aliens visit Earth

3 A popstar

3 A scientist

3 An astronaut

UNDER THE SEA 1

2 There's a huge concert

3 A Premier League footballer

3 You

3 There's a massive game of hide and seek

AN ISLAND 1

3 A unicorn

3 A zombie

2

MEEPCITY 1

2 Someone orders pizza

3 Piggy

Everyone on Earth gets superpowers

An old treasure map is found

2 **ROYALE HIGH 1**

A PIZZA PARLOUR 1

2

The rest is up to you!

ROBLOX

4

GET CREATIVE!

HOW TO BOSS THE BLOX

WANT TO BE A ROBLOX CHAMPION? FOLLOW THESE TOP T...

1 WATCH AND LEARN

If you're not sure how to beat a game, stand back and watch how the others do it – they might show you a hidden trick!

2 KEEP AN EYE ON YOUR STATS

Whether it's HP, time, or even hunger bars, don't forget to watch your stats!

House Finch

3 GET AN AWESOME AVATAR

Make yourself stand out by dressing your avatar out in cool clothes, hairstyles, and even animal companions from the catalog!

Our fave avatar is Pua from Moana. We love that pig!

4 A GOOD VIEW

You can find your opponents quickly by climbing up high and looking around, then you can hunt them down in Hide and Seek or with your sniper rifle!

5 PLAY EVERY DAY

If you log into Roblox daily, you'll get achievements! Can you log in once a day for 20 days in a row?

6 HIDE INSIDE OBJECTS

People don't tend to look inside physical objects, so they make great hiding places!

7 PVP PRO

Turn to the left while you attack with your sword, then swing to the right – it keeps your chest protected from your rival's sword!

And when in doubt... JUMP! Whether it's to greet other players or avoid certain doom, mashing the jump button is usually a good strategy!

8 LOOK INSIDE OF FLOORS

This one isn't solid, because the camera goes right through it!

The camera can't pass through this one, so it's safe to walk on!

PIZZA THE ACTION!

■ Can you spot all five differences between these two pics?

ANSWER

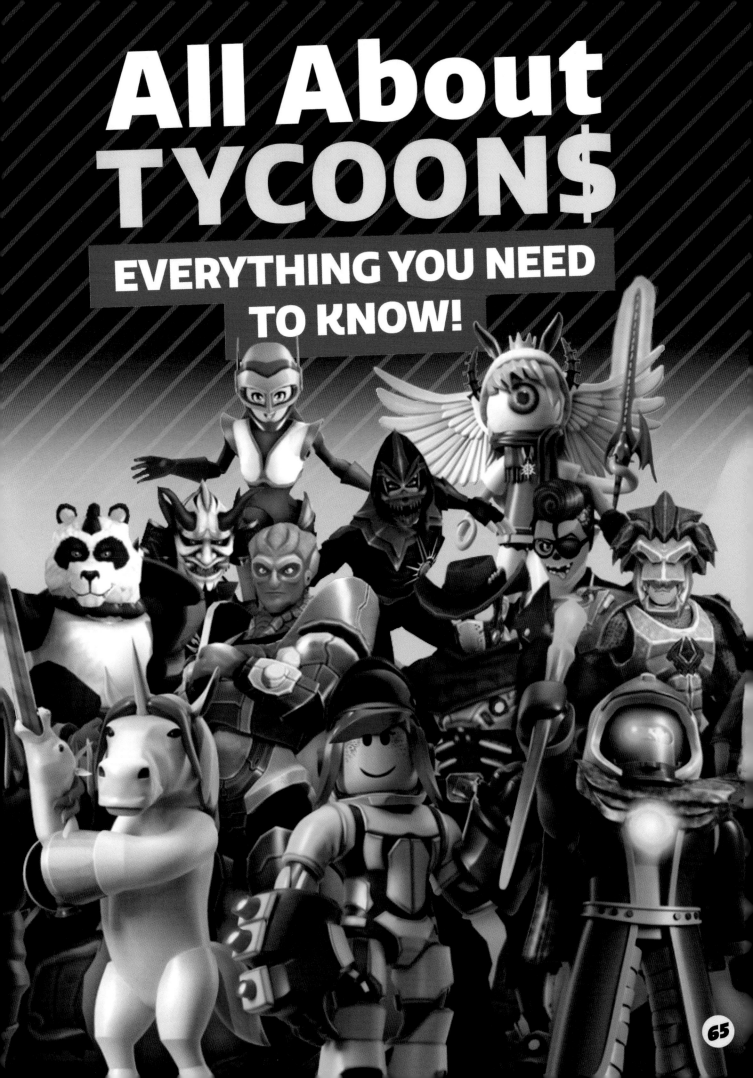

All About
TYCOON$
EVERYTHING YOU NEED TO KNOW!

WHAT IS IT?

Tycoon games are all about making money! Although there are hundreds of different tycoons available to play, most of them follow the same basic formula: start a business, make money, upgrade your equipment, make even more money – it's as easy as that!

HOW TO PLAY!

Try setting yourself some goals. If there's an item you want to save up for, think about the best way to hit your savings goal. Do you have to spend money to make money, and upgrade a bit of kit, or do you just leave your business running and go do something else until you hit your target? It's up to you!

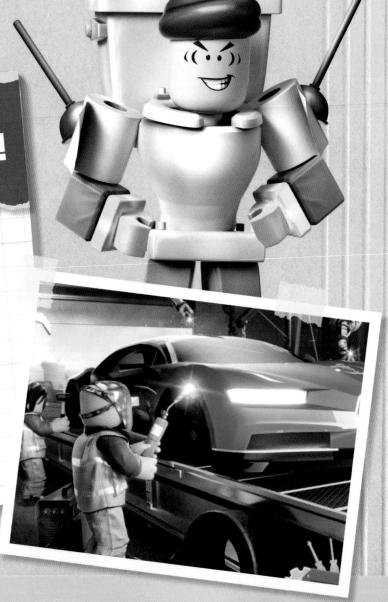

TOP TYPES!

While there are two main types of tycoon – one-player and two-player – there's loads of variety when it comes to what you can do in each game. Some tycoons simply focus on building your production line and unlocking cool items, but others are much more complex and let you build your own world!

TICK THE GAMES YOU'VE PLAYED!

UPD

GOING SOLO

Tycoons to try on your own!

- ☐ Tropical Resort Tycoon
- ☐ Car Factory Tycoon
- ☐ YouTuber Tycoon

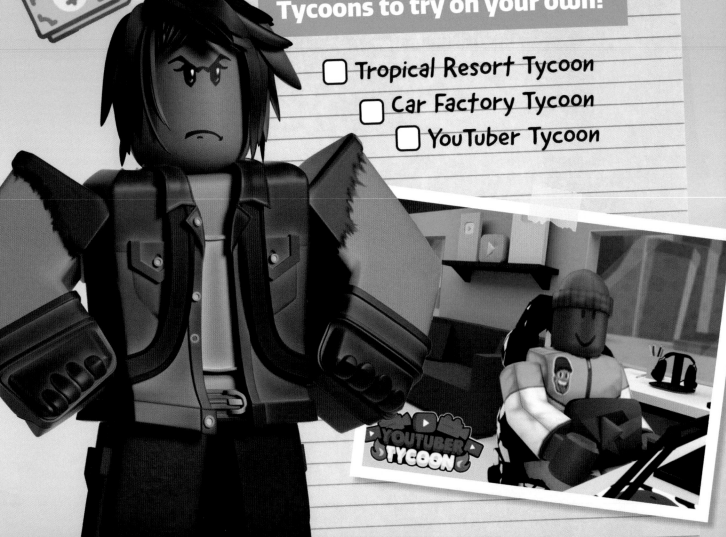

$0 $999M

NEW WIZARD TYCOON
2 Player

TEAM UP

Work together to earn big!

- ☐ 2 Player Millionaire Tycoon
- ☐ Wizard Tycoon
- ☐ 2 Player Super Hero Tycoon

POWER WASH TYCOON

MILK TYCOON

SO RANDOM

These games are so weird!

- ☐ Power Wash Tycoon
- ☐ Milk Tycoon
- ☑ Be a Spider Tycoon

WHICH TYCOON GAME ARE YOU?

Answer these questions to find out!

CHASE THAT BAG!

YOUR IDEAL DAY OUT WOULD BE...

1 Pizza and pals

2 Hanging out with fam

3 Playing the latest video game

4 SPLAT! Paint ball

5 A mega theme park

YOUR FAVOURITE SNACK IS...

1 Pizza

2 Pasta

3 Choccy bars

4 Veggies

5 Candyfloss

OH NO! THERE'S A CAT STUCK IN A TREE! DO YOU...

1 Tempt it down with a snack

2 Leave it – a cat always lands on its feet

3 Ask an adult to help

4 Climb the tree and carry it down

5 Bend the branch so it can climb down

YOUR FAVOURITE COLOUR IS...

1 Red

2 Yellow

3 Blue

4 Green

5 Purple

WORK AT A PIZZA PLACE — 4-9

You love food! Particularly pizza, arguably the best snack of all time. Your passion for pizza knows no bounds!

SUPER HERO TYCOON — 10-15

You're great at helping others but also kick serious butt too! You're the hero Roblox needs AND deserves!

THEME PARK TYCOON 2 — 16-20

You're all about the thrills! Through the highs, lows and loop-de-loops, you just want to have tons of fun!

TOP TYCOONS!

LOVE MAKING BIG BUCKS? WE RANK THE BEST TYCOON GAMES IN ROBLOX!

THEME PARK TYCOON 2

What's better than going to a theme park? Having one of your own! Get creative and even terraform your own underground rides!

OUR RATING: 9

YOUR RATING:

SUPER HERO TYCOON

Why choose one superhero?! In Super Hero Tycoon, you can play as Batman, Spider-Man, Hulk and more as you build up your epic base!

OUR RATING: 8

YOUR RATING:

RESTAURANT TYCOON 2

Hello, master chefs! Build up your kitchen and cook amazing food to tempt new customers and you could earn loads of cash!

OUR RATING: 8

YOUR RATING:

SUMMONER TYCOON

Prove you're the best! Collect and level up summons to use in battles and find epic loot along the way in Summoner Tycoon!

OUR RATING: 7

YOUR RATING:

CITY LIFE TYCOON

Think you've got what it takes to create and run your own city? Then put your Robux where your mouth is with City Life Tycoon!

OUR RATING: 6

YOUR RATING:

AWESOME!

10
9
8
7
6
GREAT
5
4
3
2
1
COOL

SPORTS ZONE

BE A SPORTING SUPERSTAR WITH THESE SUPER GAMES!

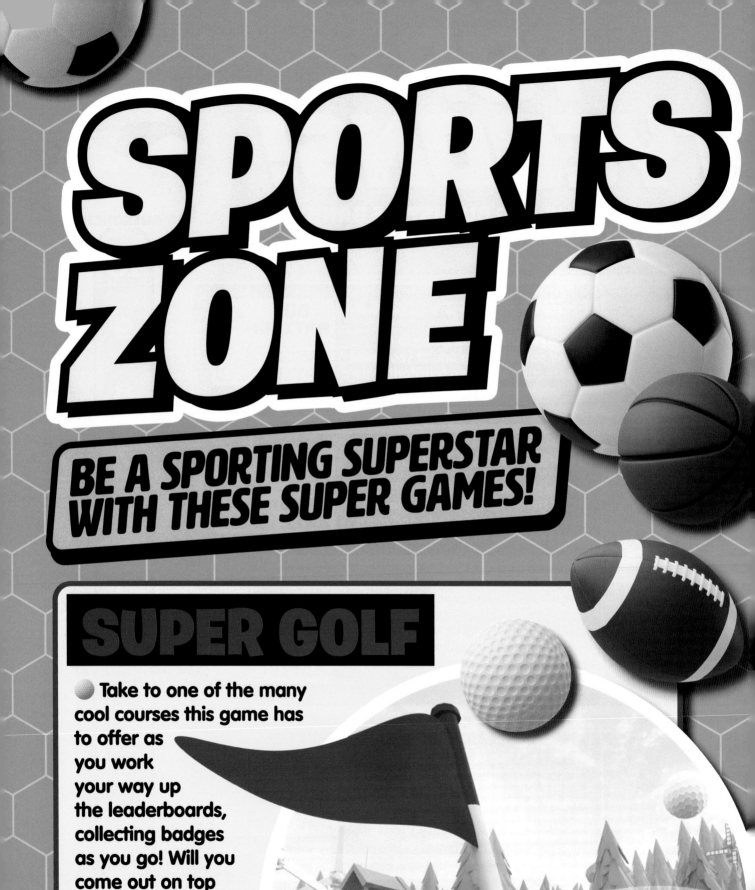

SUPER GOLF

Take to one of the many cool courses this game has to offer as you work your way up the leaderboards, collecting badges as you go! Will you come out on top with a hole in one or will you bottom out with a bogey?!

TPS: STREET SOCCER

⚽ Show off your soccer skills in style but watch out – this is no ordinary game of football! With knockouts, power shots and even superpowers, TPS: Street Soccer will put your tekkers to the test like never before.

DUNKING SIMULATOR

🏀 Shoot hoops and slam dunk your way to success on the court! There are loads of awesome jerseys to collect, balls to unlock and even shoes to earn so you can improve your gameplay, range, accuracy and focus in style!

73

FOOTBALL FUSION 2

Although some mechanics in this fast-paced football game, like passing, might be tricky to master at first, once you do, you'll be scoring touchdowns and field goals all day long! Plus, there are loads of customisation options, too. TOUCHDOWN!

DODGEBALL

Duck, dip, dodge and dive to survive in this hard-hitting game! As you battle it out in teams of six vs. six, you'll need to work together, chat to your teammates and come up with solid strategies if you want to snag that W.

SUPER STRIKER LEAGUE

⚽ It's time to take football to the extreme! With epic items to unlock and upgrade, power-ups to master and special abilities to show off, there's never a dull moment in Super Striker League – GOOOAAALLL!

JUNGLE ADVENTURE

WHAT GAME WILL YOU MASTER?

START

CHOOSE YOUR FAVE JUNGLE ANIMAL:

— GORILLA → **WHAT'S MORE IMPORTANT IN A GAME?**

— TIGER → **PICK A FRUIT:**

— ACTION →

WHAT'S MORE IMPORTANT IN A GAME?

— THE STORY → **YOU'RE ALWAYS...**

PICK A FRUIT:

— MANGO →

— PINEAPPLE → **YOU'D RATHER SLEEP IN A...**

WHAT SOUNDS MORE FUN?

— JUNGLE SAFARI → **YOU'D RATHER SLEEP IN A...**

— KAYAKING → **YOU'RE ALWAYS...**

— TREEHOUSE → **WHICH ROBLOX GAMES DO YOU PREFER?**

YOU'RE ALWAYS...

— ON TIME → **WHICH ROBLOX GAMES DO YOU PREFER?**

— IN A HURRY → **GAMES WITH MULTIPLE ENDINGS ARE...**

YOU'D RATHER SLEEP IN A...

— TENT → **WHAT BEST DESCRIBES YOU?**

WHICH ROBLOX GAMES DO YOU PREFER?

— ESCAPE OBBIES →

— TYCOONS →

GAMES WITH MULTIPLE ENDINGS ARE...

— INTERESTING → **THE JUNGLE STORY**

— NOT FOR ME → **THE JUNGLE OBBY**

WHAT BEST DESCRIBES YOU?

— ADVENTUROUS → **THE JUNGLE OBBY**

— CREATIVE → **JUNGLE TYCOON**

THE JUNGLE STORY

You're super-daring and are always up for a challenge. Making it through this interactive story game isn't easy, but we think you have what it takes!

THE JUNGLE OBBY

You're very adventurous and like games that keep you on your toes. You can do anything you put your mind to — like escaping this **Roblox** jungle!

JUNGLE TYCOON

You've got the patience and creativity needed to design your own tropical jungle. It'll be hard work but will be worth it in the end!

EVERYTHING YOU NEED TO KNOW ABOUT
ADOPT ME!

GAMER, WE'VE GOT YOU COVERED!

GOOD VIBES

It doesn't matter if you're a hardcore gamer or only play every now and again, Adopt Me! has something for everyone. There's more to this Roblox game than just looking after pets, you can also explore and customise your own home.

PERFECT PETS

Part of the fun is having pets like penguins, dragons and unicorns that you can't have IRL! Hatch eggs by trading for or buying them at the Nursery.

TOP TIP!

Like ACNH, you'll get rewarded for logging in every day. This is an easy way to earn Bucks to spend on in-game items like gifts, eggs, and toys!

IF YOU LIKE ADOPT ME!, YOU'LL LOVE THESE GAMES!

LITTLE FRIENDS: DOGS & CATS

Nintendo Switch

STAR STABLE

PC, Mobile

VIVA PIÑATA

PC, Xbox

ZOO TYCOON

PC, XBI, XBSX/S

AWESOME ANIMALS!

AWESOME!

NINJA MONKEY

■ Ninja Monkey could only be adopted during an event in 2020, and is obviously the coolest creature in the Adopt Me! game. To get him back then, players had to collect three scrolls and a monkey. If you want him now, you'll have to trade for him!

OUR RATING: 10

YOUR RATING: ☐

LAVENDER DRAGON

■ If you can get your hands on a Lavender Dragon, you won't be disappointed. It's a cool purple and white dragon that can learn to dance! It also changes colour at night!

OUR RATING: 9

YOUR RATING: ☐

GIRAFFE

■ The long-necked Giraffe could only be obtained from a Safari Egg that's no longer available. It is very cute and there are even neon versions so if you want one, you better get trading!

OUR RATING: 7

YOUR RATING: ☐

PEACOCK

■ The Peacock is a very cool blue bird with a lot of big tail feathers with orange accents. It's one of the only creatures in Adopt Me! that doesn't have to grow extra wings when it is flown by a player.

OUR RATING: 6

YOUR RATING: ☐

QUEEN BEE

■ Players can adopt a Bee at the Coffee Shop in Adopt Me! at any time, but what makes the Queen Bee a bit cooler is that there is only a 2.5% chance of it being a Queen. If you have one, you've been really lucky!

OUR RATING: 6

YOUR RATING: ☐

10
9
8
7
6 GREAT
5
4
3
2
1 COOL

UNICORN'S DIARY!

WHAT A LEGENDARY DAY!

7AM ◼ It's morning! I'll have to get up soon and start horsing around. For most people that's a bad thing, but when you're a unicorn people are OK with it.

BE MORE UNICORN!

10AM ◼ Let's head outdoors and explore Adoption Island. Maybe I'll go to the Playground first, then treat myself to something awesome at the Hat Shop!

2PM ◼ I've been practising my Backflip trick. I'm getting good at it. I barely ever land on my face now! Ow. Nevermind. Just did.

6PM ◼ I bumped into the Evil Unicorn at the Campfire. It was so dark I almost didn't notice him – good job he's got such spooky red eyes that glow in the dark!

9PM ◼ Getting a bit sleepy, but it's hard to nod off when the Neon Unicorn is lighting up the entire street like a disco! I wonder if she has a dimmer switch somewhere...

ROYALE HIGH

COOL SCHOOL!

THE GAME:

School...
but you're
magical!

ROYALS RULE!

THE EXTRAS:

▶ Classes to attend and learn.

▶ A house to live in and have fun.

▶ Outfits to make you look like royalty!

HOT TIPS:

HOW LOW CAN YOU GO?!

A fun way to earn diamonds is by going to the disco and doing the cool limbo minigame! You will gain some sweet rewards if you can complete it!

SET A REMINDER!

You can unlock cool prizes like diamonds and items by logging in every day. To help you remember this, you could set a reminder on your phone or a sticky note on the fridge!

NIGHTY NIGHT!

When your energy is low, make sure you head to the bed in your house asap, as when you gain the energy, you also gain XP! This also allows you to have a little short break from the intense life of a prince or princess!

RATINGS

Colour in your stats for Royale High.

COOLNESS	
SKILL	
FUN	
OVERALL	

WHO WINS? YOU DECIDE

BROOKHAVEN

BRILL BUILDS!

BROOKHAVEN

THE GAME:

A neighbourhood... where you can do anything!

BROOK BFFS!

THE EXTRAS:

▶ Toys and accessories to play with.

▶ Tough trophies to earn.

▶ Fantastic furniture to unlock and decorate.

HOT TIPS:

EXPLORE!

Looking for something to do? The world is filled with secrets and cool areas for you to find! Take a look around and solve puzzles; maybe you will be surprised at what you have found!

LOCK THE DOORS!

If people keep breaking into your house and messing around with your stuff, don't panic! Make sure you lock the doors when you are out and about or when you're inside so that only people you want to enter can!

TIME FOR A MAKEOVER!

If you're playing the role of a doctor, wearing a silly outfit just won't cut it! You can customise your character for free by pressing the avatar editor button in the game!

RATINGS

Colour in your stats for Brookhaven.

COOLNESS

SKILL

FUN

OVERALL

WOULD YOU RATHER...

YOU CAN ONLY PICK ONE!

ESCAPE A HORDE OF ZOMBIES

OR

RUN AWAY FROM A WEREWOLF?

HAVE A ROBLOX PET IRL

OR

EAT ROBLOX FOOD IRL?

GRUB'S UP!

BUILD AN AWESOME SUPERHERO BASE

OR

DRIVE THE SPORTS CAR OF YOUR DREAMS?

AVOID A FLOOR OF LAVA

OR

MAKE IT TO THE TOP OF THE MOUNTAIN IN AVALANCHE?

SKYWARS

NOOOOOOOO!

SKYWARS

If you're a master of Minecraft, then you'll have fun facing off with friends and foes in the Roblox game, SkyWars!

You can even set up your own private VIP server to play with your pals!

Build the biggest bases with brand-new blocks, mine for materials and destroy anyone who gets in your way until you're the strongest one in the skies!

PLAY NOW!

● There are lots of versions of SkyWars on Roblox, but 16bitplay Games's version is our fave to play with friends!

GAME SEARCH!

Can you find your fave Roblox games?

```
X W B S N K Z T I Q K G B U E O B G T R
A R O Y A L E H I G H H T K E E T J F N
Y E Z R B X H E P Z A V W A K L F E D W
N F T E M J U E E C F M I N H S R A F K
O Q K U Y A A G J Z Z P Z V O U G T E W
A D K U Y I D G M B X Z E G U O I Q G B
Z T D N N L K C V M Q X S S O U S Y Q W
G V X R N B D R I T Z R U N R F W G B L
B Y J G Y R M N A T C U O D E D J J O L
L H F F D E O H V I Y G N S B Y W V O O
O J U V H A E A Y H O S J P K L J N G E
X D I M F K N K I K L Q I E A W F G A M
B R T J B C E D M P Z D X E Y Y L M B F
U G Z F C A A P T M P X G D D B T Q O M
R D X Z E T W Y W H N J O R Y A U W O I
G B S T Q H U N W U A E E U C N K M G C
V L R G O C T B O S R I E N T W X Q A P
S U R K F V D H H M E E P C I T Y R R T
V P R O D M B D Y X Y B M I P D C Z C I
B L O X F R U I T S J U Y X K A J M W E
```

- JAILBREAK ☐
- SPEED RUN ☐
- BLOXBURG ☐
- MEEPCITY ☐
- BOOGA BOOGA ☐
- ROYALE HIGH ☐
- MAD CITY ☐
- BLOX FRUITS ☐

ANSWER

BRILLIANT BREWS!

There are nearly 150 potions to choose from in Roblox Wacky Wizards, so we've made it easier to pick your next brew! Simply spin a pencil to reveal what your next potion should be!

YOUR WACKY WIZARDS RECIPE GUIDE!

CREEPER
Become a Creeper and the rest will be HISStory!
YOU WILL NEED:
Eggcano
Dynamite

EXPLODING SQUIRTS
This is exactly as it sounds... we wish we had goggles!
YOU WILL NEED:
Rotten Sandwich
Dynamite

GHOSTLY
Boo! Don't scare yourself when you turn into a ghost!
YOU WILL NEED:
Bird
Spider

BUZZING
Because who doesn't want bee wings!
YOU WILL NEED:
Bird
Honey

RATTY
Make all your rodent dreams come true!
YOU WILL NEED:
Spider
Witches Brew

FIREWORK
Become a firework and make Katy Perry proud!
YOU WILL NEED:
Pool Noodle
Dynamite

DISCO BODY
You ARE the party!
YOU WILL NEED:
Disco Ball
Brain
You

KABOOM
your attacks are DYNAMITE!
YOU WILL NEED:
Dynamite
Boxing Gloves

SLINKY
Become a human... well, Roblox slinky!
YOU WILL NEED:
Pool Noodle
Disco Ball

SPIDER-MAN
Sling webs and save the city!
YOU WILL NEED:
You
Spider

TIP!
ADD A POOL NOODLE TO THIS RECIPE AND SEE WHAT HAPPENS!

ROBLOX

THE HOTTEST GAMES RIGHT NOW!

10

SCUBA DIVING AT QUILL LAKE

● Explore the mysteries of the ocean and track down curious artifacts in Scuba Diving at Quill Lake. You can explore pirate coves and shark-infested waters, but make sure to avoid toxic waste!

9

ISLANDS

● Island living isn't all about relaxing! From fighting mobs to building and farming, you'll definitely be kept busy. Packed with resources to collect and items to craft, Minecraft fans will love this!

8

ROYALE HIGH

● Are you ready for your first day at Royale High? Explore the school, dress up and complete missions to level up. Plus, you can visit different realms, host friends and take part in dance competitions!

4

ADOPT ME!

● Always wanted a furry (or fanged!) friend, but your parents say no? Roblox is here to help! From dogs to dinosaurs, adopt and take care of your dream pets – or try out adopting a child or being adopted!

3

MEEPCITY

● Welcome to MeepCity! Here you can hang out and play games, go fishing, create the coolest estates, and even adopt your very own baby Meep. It's all you ever wanted from city-living!

2

WORK AT A PIZZA PLACE

● Have you not ever dreamt of working at a pizza place? No? Well, maybe you will after playing this insanely fun game! Put your teamwork to the test as you get to grips with everything pizza related!

REPLAY!

7

EPIC MINIGAMES

● These minigames really are epic – with over 100 to play, you'll never get bored! Level up every time you win and spend coins on cool effects to make your character awesome!

6

HIDE AND SEEK EXTREME

● You can run... and you can hide! If you're 'it' you can use your character's special ability to find the other players. On the flip side, can you find the best places to hide from the seeker and taunt them from afar?

5

SUPER HERO TYCOON

● Ever wanted to be Batman or Thor? Play as your favourite superhero and show your might through battle! Build the biggest, coolest base to impress your friends and family!

1 JAILBREAK

● The ultimate game of cops and robbers! Will you follow the law and capture some crafty criminals or stage a super heist and make a great escape?

STEALING THE TOP SPOT!

SPOT THE DIFFERENCE!

■ There are five sneaky differences between these two pics. Can you find them all?

ANSWER

ROCKSTAR RACERS!

RANKING THE BEST RACING GAMES IN ROBLOX!

DRIVING EMPIRE

■ The ultimate driving sim – but why just take cars for spin? Put your speedy skills to the test on a boat or a motorbike, too!

OUR RATING: 9

YOUR RATING:

DEATHRUN

■ Race your way through the tricks and traps of Deathrun's most dangerous maps to see if you've got what it takes to be a parkour pro!

OUR RATING: 8

YOUR RATING:

SPEED RUN 4

■ An oldie but a goodie, Speed Run 4 pushes your avatar's agility to the max! How far can you make it in this classic obby?

OUR RATING: 7

YOUR RATING:

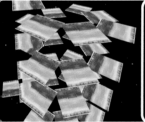

VEHICLE LEGENDS

■ Take to the roads, the seas or even the skies to race, explore and make money as you go so you can collect even more sick rides!

OUR RATING: 7

YOUR RATING:

MCLAREN F1 RACING EXPERIENCE

■ Visit the legendary HQ of the McLaren F1 team and get behind the wheel of their 2022 car in three of our fave games – Driving Simulator, Jailbreak and Ultimate Driving!

OUR RATING: 6

YOUR RATING:

AWESOME!

10
9
8
7
6
GREAT
5
4
3
2
1

COOL

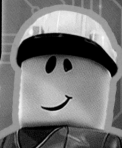

READY TO RACE!

VROOM! THESE ROBLOX RACERS ROCK!

VEHICLE LEGENDS

With cars, motorbikes, boats, planes and even helicopters, there are loads of ways to race around in style! Plus, the more you race, the more money you earn so you can buy even more epic vehicles to add to your collection.

DRIVING EMPIRE

Hit the road in this epic simulator for a driving experience that feels just like the real thing! With over 250 super-sick rides to choose from, as well as the ability to customise each car, you can really make this racer your own.

HOT WHEELS OPEN WORLD

Get the official Hot Wheels experience as you race around one of the biggest ever maps on Roblox! There are so many epic vehicles to check out, as well as loads of awesome quests to go on and epic stunts to perform!

MIDNIGHT RACING: TOKYO

Explore this epic recreation of Tokyo as you race through streets, motorways and mountains! There are over 130 different cars for you to collect and you can even tune each one to your own driving style, so you're sure to have the edge in any race.

ION FORMULA RACING

If you love Formula 1, this game is for you! Join one of 20 different teams to build and develop your own race car, competing and racing all over the world. With different weather conditions, car damage, slipstreams and more, this is one of the most realistic Roblox racers around!

MIDNIGHT RACING: TOKYO

Explore this epic recreation of Tokyo as you race through streets, motorways and mountains! There are over 130 different cars for you to collect and you can even tune each one to your own driving style, so you're sure to have the edge in any race.

ION FORMULA RACING

If you love Formula 1, this game is for you! Join one of 20 different teams to build and develop your own race car, competing and racing all over the world. With different weather conditions, car damage, slipstreams and more, this is one of the most realistic Roblox racers around!

MATCH UP MAYHEM!

Do you know your Jailbreak from your MeepCity?
Match the game to correct description!

A WELCOME TO BLOXBURG

B JAILBREAK

C ADOPT ME!

D HIDE AND SEEK EXTREME

E MEEPCITY

F ROYALE HIGH

1 Find yourself furry friends to collect and take care of!

2 This game is all about city living! Hang out or play games, or even adopt a baby Meep!

3 The ultimate game of cops and robbers! You decide what team you're on!

4 Ready or not... here I come! Get ready for an amped up version of a popular playground game!

5 It's time to go to school! Travel through realms and enter dance competitions with this jam-packed game!

6 This life-sim is perfect for players who LOVE building!

THE BEST

GAMES YOU HAVEN'T PLAYED YET!

CHECK OUT THESE FUN ROBLOX GAMES!

HERO TODAY, VILLAIN TOMORROW!

DAWN OF AURORA

In a post-apocalyptic world, a city is under siege from mutants and bandits alike! You can defend the city or play as a bandit and rob banks. Hero or villain – you decide!

TROPICAL RESORT TYCOON

Build an amazing resort on a tropical island and explore the map, find new cool things and hang out with your friends. Our favourite part is zooming about on a cool jet ski!

VOIDEL TOWERS

Climb towers and try to get to the top in the fastest time without falling. This game can be super-tricky and is great to play with friends as you compete for the best time!

ARRRGH TO THAT!

PIRATE'S FRAY

Take to the open seas and battle rival pirates on your pirate ship! This is an epic shooter game, but you can also explore islands and adopt your very own pirate pet too!

THE MATH OBBY

If you like to learn while you play, this is the game for you! Make your way through epic obstacle courses and solve fun math puzzles to get to the next level.

TERIO: HOME DESIGN BATTLE

Decorate your dream house – but with a twist! You'll be given a brief like 'crowded' or 'tropical' and must decorate your house to that style in six minutes. Then other players rate your decorating skills!

DISS MY TOILET-KITCHEN HYBRID - I DARE YOU!

95

ULTIMATE TAKE OVER!

OUR FAVE GAMES JUST GOT THE ROBLOX TREATMENT!

MINING SIMULATOR

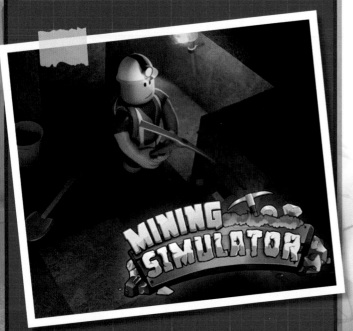

● It's time for a Minecraft-style adventure! In this epic sim, you can either team up with pals, or play solo to mine lots of valuable gems. With loads to collect and different worlds to explore, Mining Simulator is so much fun!

STRUCID

● Calling all Fortnite fans! This Roblox classic has loads of cool game modes like Free For All and Capture the Flag, as well as a sick Battle Royale Mode once you reach level 10. If you're a Fortnite boss, you'll be taking the W in no time at all!

I'M GOING FOR GOLD!

LOOMIAN LEGACY

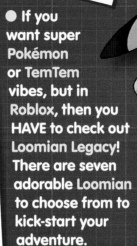

● If you want super Pokémon or TemTem vibes, but in Roblox, then you HAVE to check out Loomian Legacy! There are seven adorable Loomian to choose from to kick-start your adventure.

MEEPCITY

● Hey, Sims fans – this one's for you! Adopt your very own Meep then get exploring your neighbourhood and estate. There are loads of amazing items you can get to kit out your home in style!

SUPER STRIKER LEAGUE

● Imagine FIFA and Rocket League combined, then throw in some Roblox craziness and you've got Super Striker League! This wild game takes football to a wacky new level and it's so cool!

A GAME BY
CS CINDER STUDIO

ROBLOX AT THE MOVIES!

RO-WIZARD

- If you like Harry Potter, you'll love RO-Wizard! You can learn to become a wizard, master magical spells and go up against fantastic beasts!

TOTALLY CHARMING!

ESCAPE THE MINIONS

- This despicable obby is so much fun! Unleash your inner parkour pro as you run and jump your way through each level.

4 PLAYER SUPERHERO TYCOON

- Join a group of four heroes – or villains – to fight crime and go head-to-head with enemy teams!

STAR WARS ROGUE ONE TYCOON

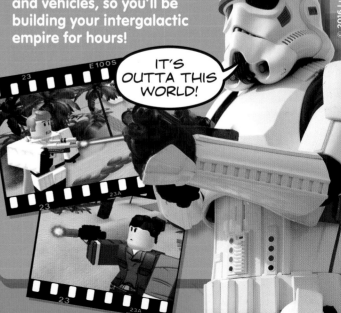

- This is the Roblox game you're looking for! It's full of cool Star Wars style characters and vehicles, so you'll be building your intergalactic empire for hours!

IT'S OUTTA THIS WORLD!

WHAT TO PLAY!

■ FOLLOW THE FLOWCHART TO FIND OUT WHICH ROBLOX GAME YOU SHOULD PLAY NEXT!

START

WHICH WORD DESCRIBES YOU BEST?

FUNNY! → **SOMEONE BURPS IN A QUIET CLASS. YOU...**

BRAVE! → **YOU'D RATHER HAVE...**

GIGGLE! → **OBBIES OR TYCOONS?**

SUPER POWERS! → **OBBIES OR TYCOONS?**

MAGIC MATES! → **RETRO GAMES ARE...**

BURP LOUDER! → **WHEN YOU GET POCKET MONEY YOU...**

SPEND IT! → **OBBIES OR TYCOONS?**

EPIC! → **RETRO GAMES ARE...**

OBBIES! → **PICK A SWEET TREAT.**

TYCOONS! → **BEST SLEEPOVER ACTIVITY?**

OLD! → **BEST SLEEPOVER ACTIVITY?**

SAVE IT! → **PICK A SWEET TREAT.**

PICK A SWEET TREAT.

BEST SLEEPOVER ACTIVITY?

POPCORN! | CANDYFLOSS! | GAMING! | MOVIES!

DRAGON ADVENTURE

● Become a dragon master! Find and raise different types of dragon, defeat enemies and even go flying in this epic game!

HEROES OF ROBLOXIA

● Team up with Captain Roblox and the squad and use your super powers to help stop crime and save the city of Robloxia!

SWORDBURST 2

● Get ready to go on an awesome adventure in this epic RPG! You can defeat enemies, collect rare items and unlock new worlds to explore!

VEHICLE SIMULATOR

● Whether you're collecting cool cars, racing your mates or even just cruising around your world, Vehicle Simulator rocks!

A-Z OF ROBLOX

A WHOLE ALPHABET OF AWESOME GAMES!

A

ADOPT ME!
All the cute pets!

B
BROOKHAVEN
Explore this amazing city!

C

CAR CRUSHERS 2
Ultimate destruction!

D

DEMONFALL
Fight to survive!

E

EMERGENCY RESPONSE: LIBERTY COUNTY
Nee naw, coming through!

F
FLEE THE FACILITY
Run away!

G

GREENVILLE
So many cool cars!

H
HIDE & SEEK EXTREME
Come out, come out, wherever you are!

I
ISLANDS

J
JAILBREAK
Goodie or baddie, your call!

K
KING LEGACY

L
LOOMIAN LEGACY
One for Pokémon fans!

M MEEPCITY
The coolest place to hang!

R ROYALE HIGH
School's never been so cool!

N NINJA LEGENDS

S STRUCID
Epic Battle Royale!

X XMAS UPDATES
All the best games get an Xmas update!

T TOWER DEFENSE SIMULATOR

O OUTLASTER
Avoid elimination!

U UK:RC REDWOOD COUNTY
Keep the world safe!

V VR HANDS
High five!

Y YOUR BIZARRE ADVENTURE
Ace RPG action!

P PIGGY

Z ZOMBIE UPRISING

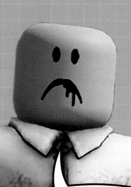

W WELCOME TO BLOXBURG
Build your own world!

Q Q-CLASH
Battle it out!

> BRRRAAAIIINS!

SUPER SPORTS!

WHICH SPORTY GAME SHOULD YOU PLAY NEXT?

Cross off the answers that sound most like you!

I'M SUPER-COMPETITIVE!

I LIKE SHOWING OFF!

I WORK BETTER ON MY OWN.

I KNOW EVERYTHING ABOUT MY FAVOURITE SPORT!

I DO WELL UNDER PRESSURE.

I WORK WELL IN A TEAM.

I'M VERY ENERGETIC.

I ALWAYS HAVE A GAME PLAN.

HAVING FUN IS MORE IMPORTANT THAN WINNING.

RESULTS

MOSTLY BLUE
SOCCER

◼ Being such an awesome team player, TPS: Soccer is the perfect pick for you. You play to win which means you always have a game plan in mind before kick-off!

MOSTLY RED
SKATE PARK

◼ You prefer doing things on your own, but that doesn't mean you can't show off! Spending hours in Skate Park mastering tricks and whizzing down ramps is your idea of fun.

MOSTLY GREEN
DODGEBALL

◼ You love sports that get your heart racing, making Dodgeball the game for you. Not only are you fearless in the arena, but you've also got a competitive streak!

LOL ZONE!

YOU'LL LAUGH YOUR RO-BUTT OFF!

Why did the football match finish early?

The players blocked off the pitch!

Why did the robot fail his exams?

He was a bit rusty!

Did you hear about the guy who got banned from Roblox?

He's blocked!

How does a ninja say hello?

Hi-Yaaaaaah!

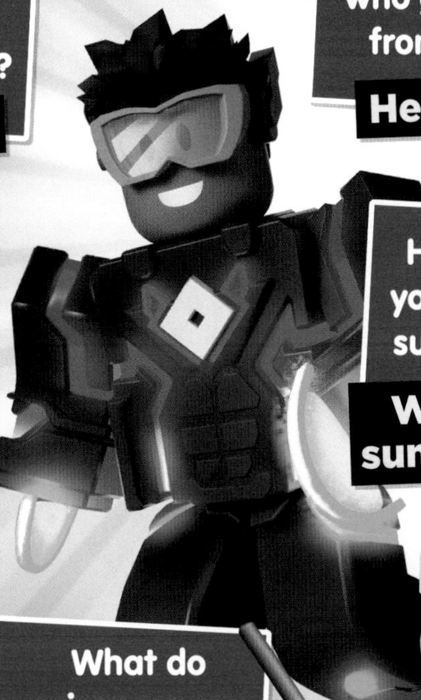

What do tycoons eat to get really rich?

Fortune cookies!

How do you avoid sunburn?

Wear sunblox!

What's the difference between a bad pizza joke and a good one?

The delivery!

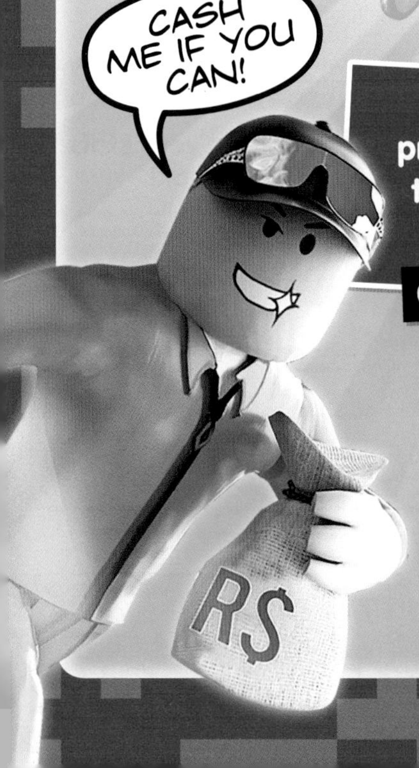

CASH ME IF YOU CAN!

What do prisoners use to call each other?

Cell phones!

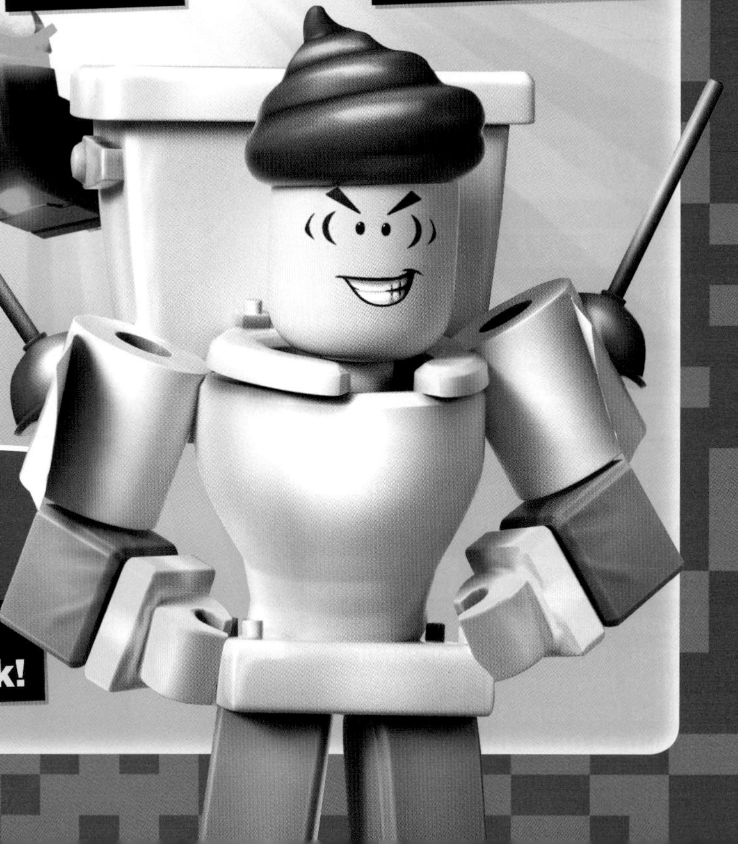

Do you want to hear a poop joke?

No, they always stink!

RS

WHO WILL WIN?

JAILBREAK

BREAK OUT!

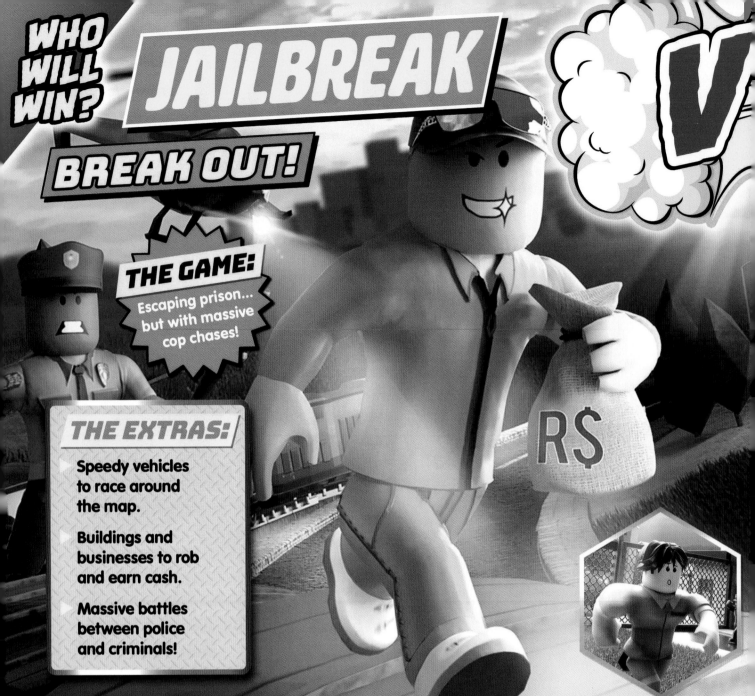

THE GAME:

Escaping prison... but with massive cop chases!

THE EXTRAS:

- Speedy vehicles to race around the map.

- Buildings and businesses to rob and earn cash.

- Massive battles between police and criminals!

HOT TIPS:

CRAWL TO VICTORY!

It might slow you down, but crawling lets you sneak under lasers, escape through vents and even makes you a harder target!

CAR THIEF!

Jailbreak is packed full of awesome vehicles, perfect for making a speedy getaway when you find yourself in a pinch!

VERY IMPORTANT PLAYER!

If you want to cause max chaos as a criminal, try out a VIP server or one with a low number of players – there'll be less cops so you can get away with so much more.

RATINGS

Colour in your stats for Jailbreak!

COOLNESS	
SKILL	
FUN	
OVERALL	

WHO WINS? YOU DECIDE!

FLEE THE FACILITY

THE GAME:

Hacking...
But with an
evil Beast!

THE EXTRAS:

▶ Customisable hammers and gems to battle in style.

▶ Skill checks to keep you on your feet.

▶ Loads of maps to explore and escape from!

HOT TIPS:

STICK TOGETHER!

Hacking all the computers on each map takes ages. If you team up with fellow players to hack the same device, you'll drastically increase the speed for completion!

GLOWING MARKER!

The loud scary music lets you know the Beast is nearby, but it doesn't tell you where they're going to appear. If you watch the walls and doors, you can spot a red glow surrounding the Beast, giving you the heads-up needed to hide!

JUMP AND SLIDE!

The Beast is faster than you, so you need to use your wits to escape! It can't go through small gaps, and jumping objects takes serious time, so when making your escape, always try to crawl through vents, jump over counters and go through windows!

RATINGS

Colour in your stats for Flee the Facility!

COOLNESS

SKILL

FUN

OVERALL

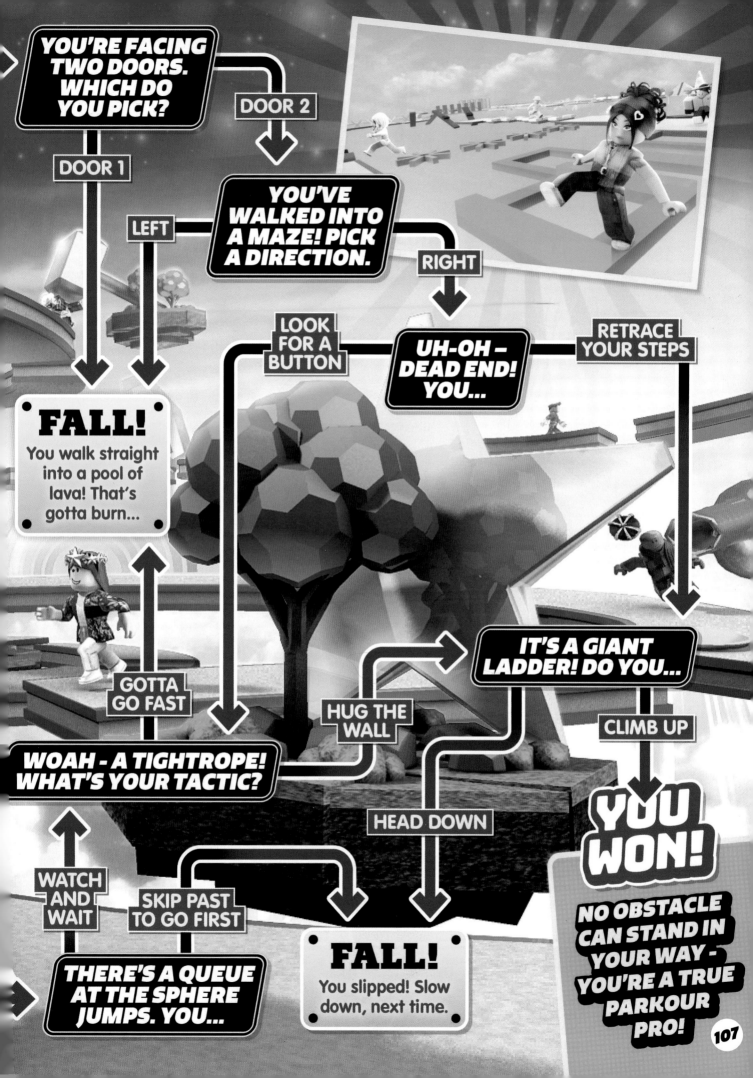

YOU'RE FACING TWO DOORS. WHICH DO YOU PICK?

DOOR 1

DOOR 2

YOU'VE WALKED INTO A MAZE! PICK A DIRECTION.

LEFT

RIGHT

LOOK FOR A BUTTON

UH-OH – DEAD END! YOU...

RETRACE YOUR STEPS

FALL!
You walk straight into a pool of lava! That's gotta burn...

GOTTA GO FAST

HUG THE WALL

IT'S A GIANT LADDER! DO YOU...

CLIMB UP

WOAH - A TIGHTROPE! WHAT'S YOUR TACTIC?

HEAD DOWN

YOU WON!

WATCH AND WAIT

SKIP PAST TO GO FIRST

THERE'S A QUEUE AT THE SPHERE JUMPS. YOU...

FALL!
You slipped! Slow down, next time.

NO OBSTACLE CAN STAND IN YOUR WAY - YOU'RE A TRUE PARKOUR PRO!

PATH PICKER!

CHOOSE A NUMBER AND FOLLOW THE PATH TO FIND OUT WHICH ADVENTURE AWAITS!

1 2 3 4

TREASURE QUEST

You'll fight all kinds of evil monsters to loot the treasure they're guarding. Want powerful new gear? Defeat the boss protecting the final treasure room!

ROBOT 64

Beebo the robot is on a quest to destroy the sun! Your unusual mission will take you through wacky worlds, with collectibles to find and puzzles to solve.

LITTLE WORLD

You have what it takes to climb the food chain! Starting off as a cute ladybug, you'll evolve by exploring, training, and collecting fruit.

WORLD ZERO

Think Dungeons and Dragons but make it Roblox! Are you brave enough to battle through different worlds and defeat fearsome bosses?